Facing Mighty Fears
About Trying New Things

Dr. Dawn's Mini Books About Mighty Fears
By Dawn Huebner, PhD
Illustrated by Liza Stevens
Helping children ages 6–10 live happier lives

Facing Mighty Fears About Animals
ISBN 978 1 78775 946 6
eISBN 978 1 78775 947 3

Facing Mighty Fears About Throwing Up
ISBN 978 1 78775 925 1
eISBN 978 1 78775 926 8

Facing Mighty Fears About Health
ISBN 978 1 78775 928 2
eISBN 978 1 78775 927 5

Watch for future titles in the
Dr. Dawn's Mini Books About Mighty Fears series.

Facing Mighty Fears About Trying New Things

Dawn Huebner, PhD

Illustrated by Liza Stevens

Jessica Kingsley Publishers
London and Philadelphia

First published in Great Britain in 2022 by Jessica Kingsley Publishers
An imprint of Hodder & Stoughton Ltd
An Hachette Company

1

Front cover image source: Liza Stevens.

A CIP catalogue record for this title is available from the British Library and the Library of Congress

ISBN 978 1 78775 950 3
eISBN 978 1 78775 951 0

Printed and bound in Great Britain by TJ Books Limited

Jessica Kingsley Publishers' policy is to use papers that are natural, renewable, and recyclable products and made from wood grown in sustainable forests. The logging and manufacturing processes are expected to conform to the environmental regulations of the country of origin.

Jessica Kingsley Publishers
Carmelite House
50 Victoria Embankment
London EC4Y 0DZ

www.jkp.com

Grown-ups:

Need ideas about how to use this book?

Please see Dr. Dawn's

Note to Parents and Caregivers

on page 67.

You'll also find a **Resource Section**

highlighting books, websites, and organizations

for parents of anxious kids.

If you were getting a present and you got to choose between two boxes—one the size and shape of a toy you like, the other a mystery—which would you choose?

If you had two plates in front of you—one with a food you've eaten many times, the other a food you've never tried—which would you choose?

FUN FACT
Koalas eat only one kind of food—eucalyptus leaves—which are fibrous and not very nutritious. This means they have to sleep 22 hours a day, to conserve energy. Imagine eating only one kind of food and then needing to lie in bed all day to digest it. Boring!

FUN FACT
Giant pandas have a limited diet, too. They eat only bamboo, which is low in nutrients. So, giant pandas must find, chew, and swallow 80 pounds (36kg) of bamboo every day. That's like eating 24,000 pretzel twists over the course of a day. You'd get sick of them, wouldn't you?

If your family was taking a trip and you got to decide where to go—the place you went last year or someplace new—which would you choose?

Chances are good you'd go with:

- → The toy you know
- → The food you know
- → The place you know

Why is that? Why do we prefer the things that we know?

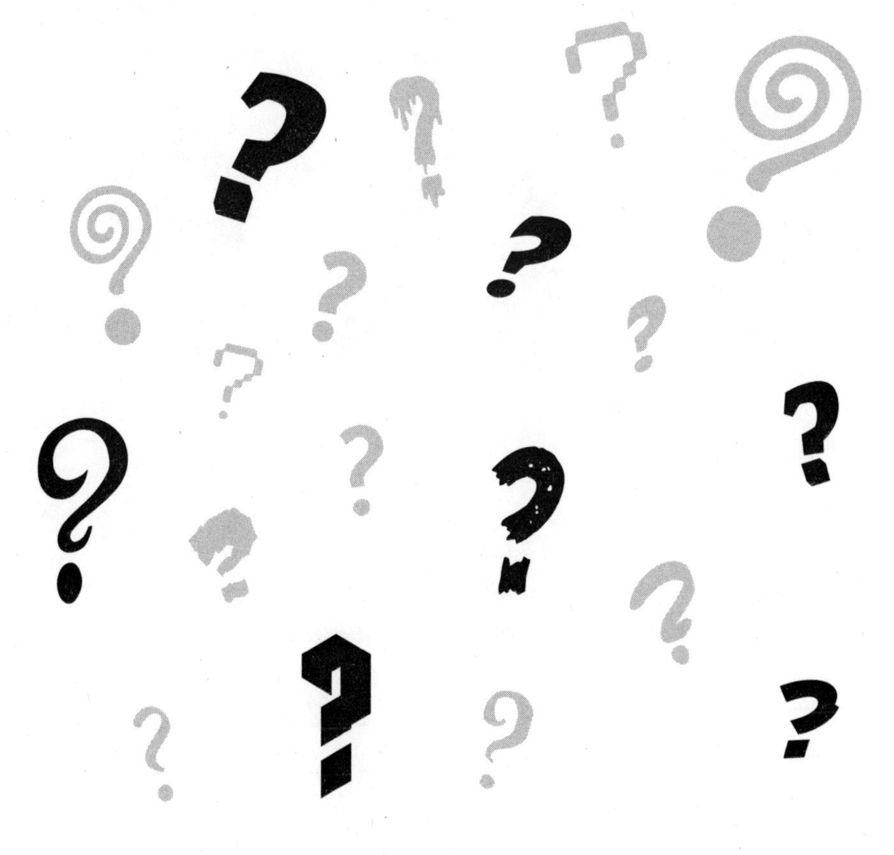

The answer is obvious, isn't it?

We prefer the things we know simply because we know them!

Choosing the unknown feels risky.

If you prefer things that you know and are cautious about things that are new, you're in good company.

Lots of people spend time with the same friends, eat the same foods, enjoy the same hobbies, and stick to the same routines...day after day after day.

FUN FACT
People used to eat peanut butter on bread, and jam on bread, but no one ever ate peanut butter AND jam on bread. The first person to try this most unusual (but now super common) combination was Julia Davis Chandler in 1901. Aren't you glad she was willing to try something new?!

FUN FACT
The first person to combine peanut butter and chocolate was Harry Burnett Reese. That was a bold experiment, too!

In fact, from the very earliest of times, humans have been wary of new experiences.

Wary (adjective)
To be cautious about possible danger; to remain alert.

That makes sense because three hundred thousand years ago—when scientists think the first humans appeared—the earth was a dangerous place.

There were no seat belts
or bike helmets
or stair railings
or shin pads.

No leashes
or flashlights
or hand sanitizer
or cell phones.

There were none of the conveniences we now count on to keep ourselves safe.

What there were, instead, were boggy marshes to get stuck in, prowling animals to get eaten by, and vast stretches of land without street signs (or streets).

To stay safe, early humans had to be aware of their surroundings, always thinking about what might happen next.

When these early humans came across something well known, it was easy to predict what would happen next:

A rabbit would always act like a rabbit.

Low dark clouds would always bring rain.

But when these early humans encountered something new, there was no way of knowing what would happen.

Would a path they had never taken lead somewhere useful, or would it end in a dangerous bog?

Would the berries on a bush they had never seen before be delicious, or would they be poisonous?

Not knowing meant taking a chance, and chances were risky because there was danger all around.

Being cautious helped these early humans survive.

We live in modern times, safer times, but we are related to these early humans. Our brains are similar to theirs.

Just like them, we have a built-in wariness about new experiences. We tend to think that new = dangerous because we don't know what to expect.

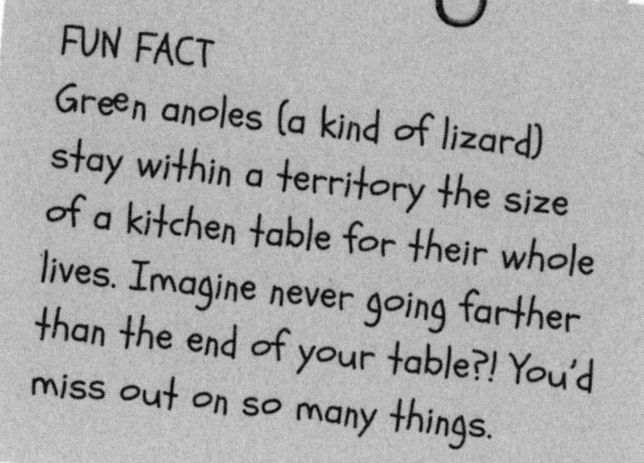

When we are faced with something new, we find ourselves wondering:

What's going to happen?

What if something goes wrong?

What if there's a problem?

Some people shrug off these questions.

But for others, the questions get magnified, and lots of what-if thoughts come crashing in.

If you are hesitant to try new things, chances are good that you have a brain magnifier.

Your brain sends out alerts when you encounter something new:

"Hey, be careful!"

"You've never done this before."

"Something might go wrong."

What-if thoughts quickly follow:

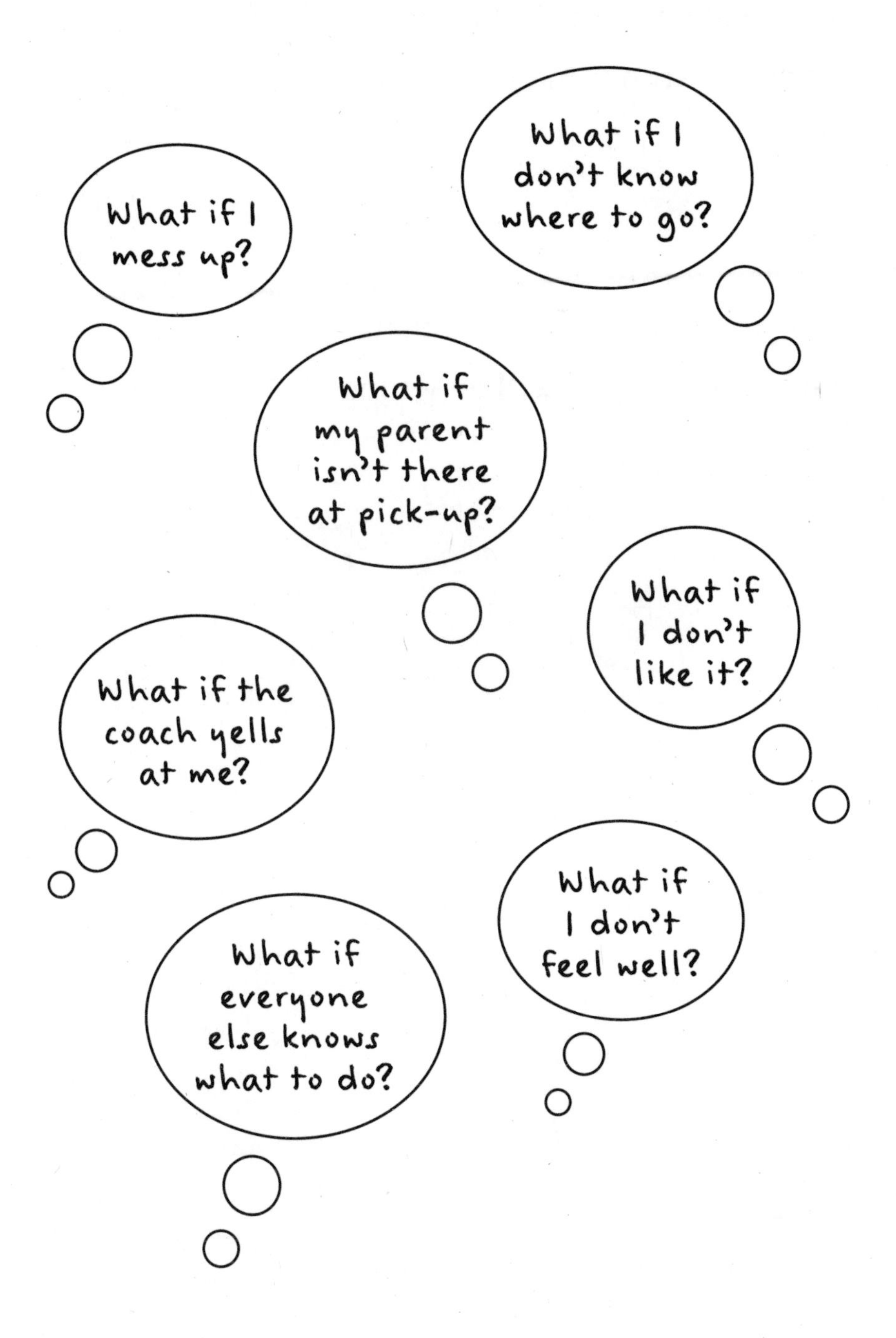

Magnifying brains are quick to recognize all the things that might go wrong, and how awful those things would be.

It begins to seem that if something **could** go wrong, it **will** go wrong.

So, when someone wants you to do something new, you are likely to say…

…because you feel nervous, and you aren't willing to risk having one of those terrible things come true.

On the other hand, you might not feel nervous at all.

You might feel angry, instead. Or bored. Or frustrated that people are pushing you to do something you don't want to do.

So, you might say:

Whether you say "no" directly or indirectly, it's important to understand that your brain is trying to protect you.

It's making you think that if you don't do the new thing—whatever that new thing is—the bad stuff you are imagining won't happen.

And then, as soon as you decide that you aren't going to do the new thing—presto!—you feel better. All your uncomfortable feelings go away.

Nervous

Apprehensive

Uncomfortable

Annoyed

Unsure

SCARED

Worried

Unsettled

But here's the thing:

The bad stuff is unlikely to happen, anyway.

Just because you are nervous doesn't mean you are in danger.

Think of a time you were nervous.

It might be a time you were facing something new, and you didn't want to do it, but you did it anyway, and it worked out fine. Maybe even GREAT.

FUN FACT
Wayne Gretzky, a Canadian considered by many to be the greatest player in the National Hockey League, said, "You miss 100 percent of the shots you don't take."

FUN FACT
Moses Fleetwood Walker was the first African American man to play for a major-league baseball team.

That's often what happens.

New experiences feel risky, but once we get started—and especially after we get used to the newness—they almost always work out fine.

So, the trick is to figure out how to move past your brain alarm and try new things, even though they make you nervous.

QUESTION: Do you remember the first tooth you lost? What about the eighth tooth? Why do you remember one more than the other?

QUESTION: Do you remember your first day of school? What about your 52nd day? Why is it hard to remember your 52nd day?

QUESTION: Do you remember the first time you tried what is now your favorite food? Was it easy or hard to try it that first time? Why?

QUESTION: Do you remember meeting your best friend? What would be different about your life if you hadn't played with them that first time?

There are three steps that can help.

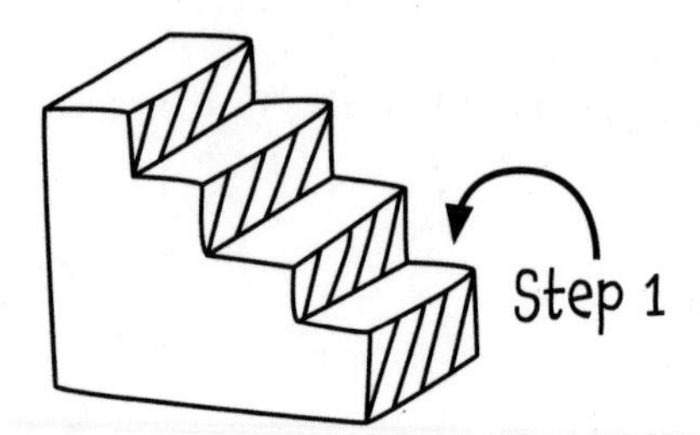

1. Ask the magic question.

When you are faced with a new experience, and you feel nervous about it, and find yourself thinking, "I don't want to do that," ask yourself:

You will quickly see that most of the foods, outings, experiences, and activities you are reluctant to try are simply new.

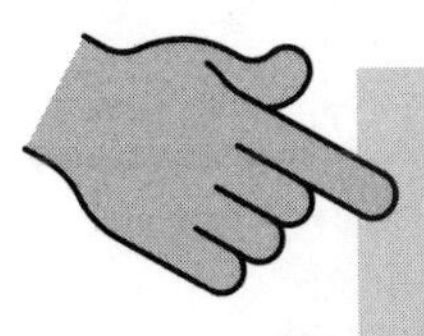

Reluctant (adjective)

Showing doubt and unwillingness.

You are uncomfortable because you don't know what to expect.

But being uncomfortable is different from being in danger.

Remind yourself:

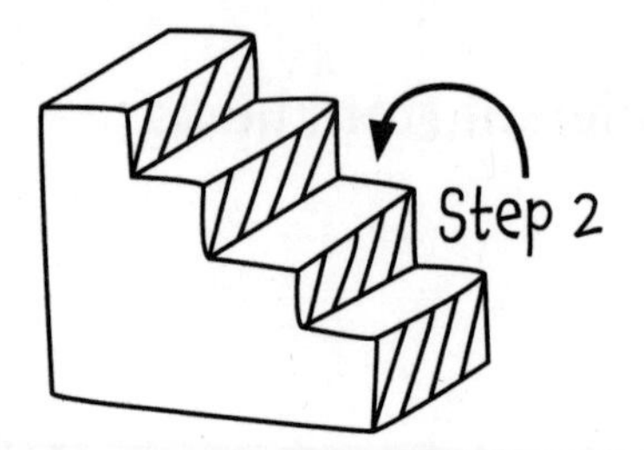

2. Focus on the facts.

Facts are things you know for sure.

Not what **might** be true or what **could** be true but what **is** true.

Worries are not facts. They are scary what-if thoughts your brain thinks up.

So, you need to turn down the volume on those thoughts. Remind yourself:

That's just my brain
what-iffing again.
I don't need to listen.

Take some deep breaths to settle your brain, then focus on the things you know to be true:

→ Big bad things are unlikely.

→ Small bad things are manageable.

When you are nervous about something new, your brain zeros in on the things you don't know.

Flip this around by paying attention to what you *do* know.

Chances are good that you know **something** about the new situation you are facing.

For example, you might know how to run, even though you've never been on a track team.

You might know what peas, chicken and potatoes taste like, even though you've never had them together in a stew.

You definitely know that you like your friend, even though you've never been to their house.

If an experience is entirely new and you don't know anything at all, it's okay to ask questions:

Who's going to be there?

Where is this?

Is it like anything I've done before?

What do you think I'll like about it?

Listen to the answers.

Remind yourself that you don't need to know every single thing.

Then, focus on the parts you do know, rather than the parts you don't know.

Your brain will settle down and you'll feel better.

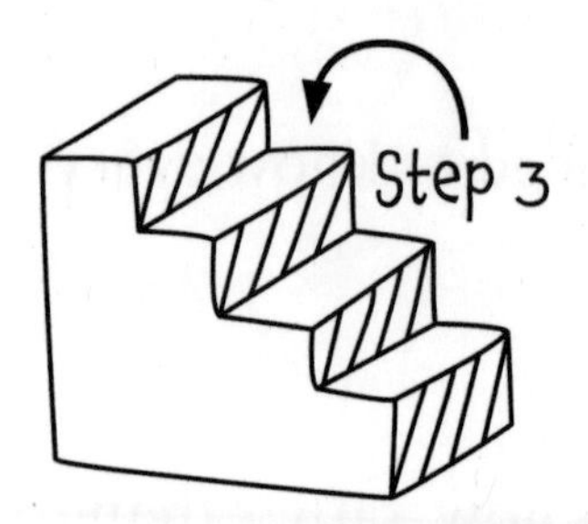

3. Practice being brave.

Being brave means feeling nervous and moving forward anyway.

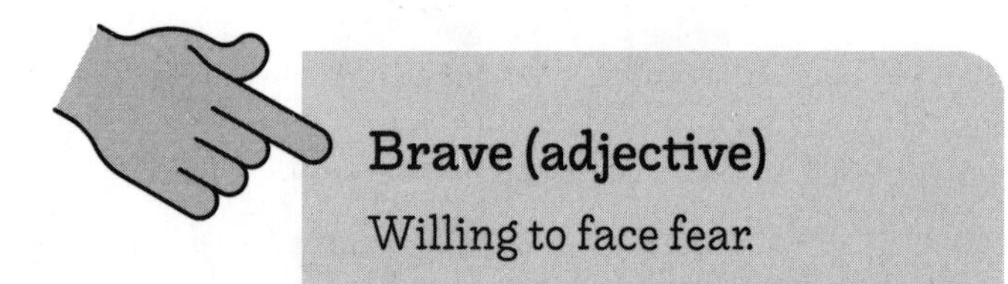

And there's some good news: you don't have to **feel** brave to **be** brave!

In fact, people who act bravely often feel quite nervous inside. But they've decided not to let their nervousness stop them.

FUN FACT
Eleanor Roosevelt, married to US President Franklin D. Roosevelt, was the first presidential spouse to use her influence to help other people. An advocate for human rights, she famously said, "Do one thing that scares you every day," and made it a point to live by her motto.

FUN FACT
Theodore Roosevelt, US President and uncle to Eleanor Roosevelt, once said, "It is hard to fail, but it is worse never to have tried."

Bravery is like a muscle.

Using it makes it stronger.

The best way to practice bravery is to challenge yourself to do one new thing every day.

That's it. Just one new thing:

Eat a single blueberry (if you've never eaten a blueberry before).

Wear mismatched socks (if you've never worn mismatched socks before).

Try a backwards somersault (if you've only done front rolls before).

Sit in a different spot
in the lunchroom.

**Write with your
eyes closed.**

Try a different
type of cereal.

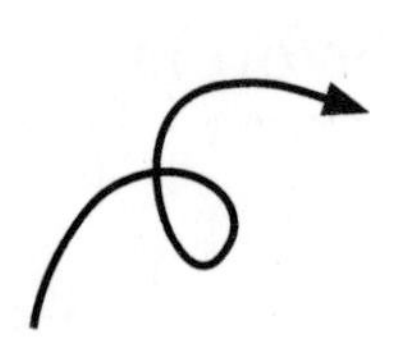

*Say hello to someone
you've never greeted.*

Learn a new card game.

Eat dinner backwards—
dessert first!

*Put your parent to bed,
then go to sleep yourself.*

Take a walk somewhere you are likely to see other people. Smile at every person you see.

Be the one to place your family's order at a carry-out restaurant.

Call or send a text to a friend you've never called or texted before.

Eat a meal with foods from every color of the rainbow.

Go to the library and choose a book you've never read before, or a book from a section you've never visited (non-fiction, biography, etc.).

Brush your teeth with the hand you don't normally use.

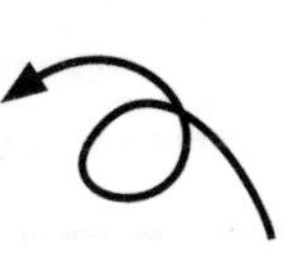

With a sibling or a friend, sit a few rows in front of your parents at a movie theatre.

Play with someone different from the person you usually play with at recess.

Try a food that children in a different part of the world like but that you've never eaten.

Invite a friend to sleep over at your house. A few weeks later, go sleep at their house. Stay all night, even if you feel nervous.

Sign up for an after-school activity you haven't done before.

Set up a tent, if you have one, or build a fort with blankets in a room other than your bedroom. Sleep in the tent (or fort) on your own. Stay there all night.

Let your parent pick a movie for you to watch, one you've never seen and don't know much about.

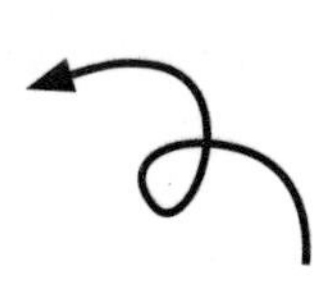

Go on a mystery outing—no questions allowed! Your parent will know where you are going, but you won't. Once you get there, find three things that are interesting or fun about the place.

Go to a playground you've never been to. See if you can get someone to play with you by playing near them or asking them to play.

Wear your hair in a different style from how you normally wear it. Keep it that way all day.

Ask your teacher a personal question such as, "Did you have pets when you were my age?"

The size of your new thing doesn't matter.

Small Medium Large

What matters is that you choose to do it, even though it makes you nervous; that you step towards the new thing without putting up a fuss or waiting for your parents to force you.

Your bravery will grow best if you decide on your own:

Even if your new things are small, big things will start to happen.

The part of your brain that has been shying away from new experiences will quiet down, and the part of your brain ready for challenge and adventure will grow stronger.

So, that's it for the three steps.

There's just one more thing to remember:

Everything you love—every food, every game, every activity, every restaurant, every park, every friend—was once new.

If you never took a chance, never, ever did anything new, you wouldn't know and love any of those things because you wouldn't have tried them.

Life would be boring.

There's so much you would miss out on.

So, when you feel nervous about doing something new, use your three steps:

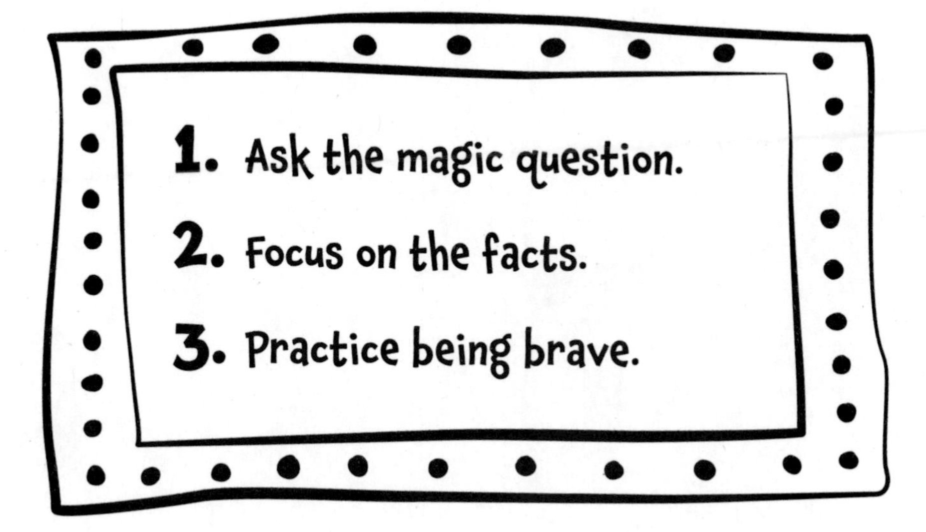

You can do it!

And then you can get on with your life.

Note to Parents and Caregivers

"I don't want to."

"No!"

"I don't like soccer… strawberries…swimming…going out to eat… [fill in the new experience of your choice here]."

Does your child sign up for new activities, then balk when it's time to go? Does she insist she doesn't like foods, or sports, or pastimes she's never tried? Does he cry, or argue, or shrink away from seemingly routine challenges, stymied by uncertainty? It's heartbreaking (and maddening) to see your child locked in a struggle between wanting and dreading, unable to step into experiences you are quite sure they will be able to manage—and enjoy—if only they would try.

Anxiety around new experiences is common. We're actually hard-wired for it, and for good reason. When faced with something new, we don't know what to expect, so our brains send out messages telling us to pay attention. But being aware that something is new, and feeling immediately averse to it simply because it is new, are two different things. We want the former (awareness), but not the latter (reflexive aversion).

For some children, gentle encouragement is enough. For others, encouragement backfires and parents find themselves ping-ponging between bargaining and forcing, eventually throwing up their hands in defeat, allowing their children to bow out. What else can a parent do?

It turns out that there is a middle path between trying to make your child do something and giving up entirely, a middle path that begins with stepping out of the specific struggle (about gymnastics, or a new kind of pasta, or whatever it is you are trying to get your child to try) and looking at the pattern.

Facing Mighty Fears About Trying New Things normalizes apprehension about new experiences while teaching specific strategies to move past it. Read this book with your child, encouraging them to map their own experiences onto the pages. Pause to enjoy the "fun facts" scattered throughout the book. Challenge your child to do the first-time acts (new things), too.

Spend time talking about the three action steps described in the book, understanding that your child will need help practicing them. Be patient and persistent. Chances are good that you and your child have a well-honed dance in which it has somehow become your job to convince your child to do something (by explaining, bargaining, coaxing, reassuring, and ultimately either forcing or backing down). It's going to take time and effort to change the pattern.

As you begin, please note that this book is geared towards children reluctant to try new things simply because they are new. It does not address the fear of making mistakes, which sometimes lies at the core of refusal. If your child struggles more widely with anxiety, you might consider using this book in combination with therapy. And if your child's anxiety triggers your own, you will undoubtedly benefit from the steady presence of a therapist to guide you.

Some additional tips

1. Make trying new things part of your family's ethos. Have everyone talk about "something new I tried today" or create a giant poster each family member can contribute to. Keep it positive. Bravery is an admirable attribute, not a chore. Celebrate adventure, willingness, and effort, regardless of how things turn out.

2. Be aware of your child's "comfort zone." Then imagine a "growth zone" just beyond it. Your goal is to teach your child to move past apprehension and uncertainty, to take one small step into their growth zone. When a child does this often enough, it becomes routine.

3. Break challenges into small steps. Rehearse them with your child. It is far better for a child to successfully take a small step than to "fail" at a larger one. If your child balks, use the language of steps. You might say, "That's a big step, let's think of a smaller one." Avoid all-or-nothing thinking. Even small steps signal progress.

4. Stay calm in the face of your child's big feelings. Remember that anger is often a cover for fear. Empathize with your child, neither pushing past nor capitulating to their feelings. You'll

find additional resources about helping children manage big feelings at the back of this book.

5. Remember that much of your child's apprehension is related to uncertainty. Normalize this. Help your child gather information, remembering that facts mitigate fears. At the same time, know that not all questions can be answered, and that needing to know every detail with absolute certainty is part of a broader anxiety pattern.

6. Be playful. Teach your child to imagine the "best case" scenario. Play the "what if" game in reverse, concocting outrageous, fanciful, wonderful possibilities. Laughing releases tension and relieves fear, making it more possible to move forward.

7. Refer back to the three steps often. They are the key to breaking free of the pattern your child is in.

You can do this. Your child can do this. I'll be rooting for you.

Dr. Dawn

Resources

Organizations

These organizations provide information about childhood anxiety, and include therapist locators to assist with finding specialized care:

USA

The Anxiety and Depression Association of America:
https://adaa.org

The International OCD Foundation:
https://iocdf.org

UK

Anxiety UK:
www.anxietyuk.org.uk

Young Minds:
https://youngminds.org.uk

AU/NZ

Beyond Blue:
www.beyondblue.org.au

Kids Health:
https://kidshealth.org.nz

Please also reach out to your child's pediatrician for names of local providers.

Web-based resources

https://library.jkp.com
Dr. Dawn's Seven-Step Solution for When Worry Takes Over: Easy-to-Implement Strategies for Parents or Carers of Anxious Kids, see page 76.
Video Training Course

www.anxioustoddlers.com
Natasha Daniels of AT Parenting Survival creates podcasts, blog posts, and free resources about anxiety. She also offers subscription courses, coaching, and treatment.

https://childmind.org
This NY Institute offers articles on a host of topics, including anxiety, with a unique "Ask an Expert" feature providing trustworthy, relatable advice.

https://copingskillsforkids.com
Janine Halloran provides free, easy-to-implement, child-friendly tips on calming anxiety, managing stress, and more.

https://gozen.com
Kid-tested, therapist-approved, highly effective animated videos teaching skills related to anxiety, resilience, emotional intelligence, and more.

www.worrywisekids.org
Tamar Chansky of WorryWiseKids provides a treasure-trove of information for parents of anxious children.

Recommended reading

There are many appealing, effective books to help children manage worries and fears. Please check with your preferred bookseller, who can guide you towards books particularly suited to your child's needs. Here are a few suggestions.

For younger children

What to Do When You Worry Too Much: A Kid's Guide to Overcoming Anxiety by Dawn Huebner, PhD, American Psychological Association.

Binnie the Baboon Anxiety and Stress Activity Book by Dr. Karen Treisman, Jessica Kingsley Publishers.

Hey Warrior: A Book for Kids about Anxiety by Karen Young, Little Steps Publishing.

Little Meerkat's Big Panic: A Story About Learning New Ways to Feel Calm by Jane Evans, Jessica Kingsley Publishers.

The Nervous Knight: A Story About Overcoming Worries and Anxiety by Anthony Lloyd Jones, Jessica Kingsley Publishers.

Starving the Anxiety Gremlin for Children Aged 5–9: A CBT Workbook on Anxiety Management by Kate Collins-Donnelly, Jessica Kingsley Publishers.

For older children

Outsmarting Worry: An Older Kid's Guide to Managing Anxiety by Dawn Huebner, PhD, Jessica Kingsley Publishers.

All Birds Have Anxiety by Kathy Hoopmann, Jessica Kingsley Publishers.

The Can-Do Kid's Journal: Discover Your Confidence Superpower! by Sue Atkins, Jessica Kingsley Publishers.

Can I Tell You About Anxiety? A Guide for Friends and Family by Lucy Willetts, Jessica Kingsley Publishers.

Doodle Your Worries Away: A CBT Doodling Workbook for Kids Who Feel Worried or Anxious by Tanja Sharpe, Jessica Kingsley Publishers.

Help! I've Got an Alarm Bell Going Off in My Head! How Panic, Anxiety and Stress Affect Your Body by K.L. Aspden, Jessica Kingsley Publishers.

The Panicosaurus: Managing Anxiety in Children, Including those with Asperger Syndrome by K.L. Al-Ghani, Jessica Kingsley Publishers.

Starving the Anxiety Gremlin: A CBT Workbook on Anxiety Management for Young People Aged 10+ by Kate Collins-Donnelly, Jessica Kingsley Publishers.

For parents

Anxious Kids, Anxious Parents by Dr. Reid Wilson and Lynn Lyons, Health Communications Inc.

The A–Z of Therapeutic Parenting: Strategies and Solutions by Sarah Naish, Jessica Kingsley Publishers.

The No Worries Guide to Raising Your Anxious Child by Karen Lynn Cassiday, Jessica Kingsley Publishers.

Parenting Your Anxious Toddler by Natasha Daniels, Jessica Kingsley Publishers.

Peaceful Parent, Happy Kids by Dr. Laura Markham, TarcherPerigee.

The Yes Brain: How to Cultivate Courage, Curiosity and Resilience in Your Child by Dr. Dan Siegel and Dr. Tina Payne Bryson, Bantam Press.

Dr. Dawn's

SEVEN-STEP SOLUTION FOR WHEN WORRY TAKES OVER

Easy-to-Implement Strategies for Parents or Carers of Anxious Kids

worry has a way of turning into WORRY in the blink of an eye. This upper-case WORRY causes children to fret about unlikely scenarios and shrink away from routine challenges, ultimately holding entire families hostage. But upper-case WORRY is predictable and manageable once you understand its tricks.

This 7-video series will help you recognize WORRY's tricks while teaching a handful of techniques to help you and your child break free.

Each video contains learning objectives and action steps along with need-to-know content presented in a clear, engaging manner by child psychologist and best-selling author, Dr. Dawn Huebner. The videos are available from https://library.jkp.com.

Video One: Trolling for Danger (time 8:15)

- The role of the amygdala in spotting and alerting us to danger
- What happens when the amygdala sets off an alarm
- Real dangers versus false alarms
- Calming the brain (yours and your child's) to get back to thinking

Video Two: The Worry Loop (time 10:15)

- The "loop" that keeps Worry in place
- How to identify where your child is in the Worry Loop

Video Three: Externalizing Anxiety (time 11:41)

- Externalizing anxiety as a powerful first step
- Talking back to Worry
- Teaching your child to talk back to Worry
- Talking back without entering into a debate

Video Four: Calming the Brain and Body (time 13:36)

- Breathing techniques
- Mindfulness techniques
- Distraction techniques
- Which technique (how to choose)?

Video Five: Getting Rid of Safety Behaviors (time 15:18)

- Preparation
- The role of exposure
- Explaining exposure to your child
- Creating an exposure hierarchy

Video Six: Worrying Less Is Not the Goal (time 13:02)

- The more you fight anxiety, the more it holds on
- The more you accommodate anxiety, the more it stays
- Anxiety is an error message, a false alarm
- When you stop letting Worry be in charge, it fades

Video Seven: Putting It All Together (time 19:42)

- A review of the main techniques
- Deciding where to start
- The role of rewards
- Supporting your child, not Worry